I0816484

Our brains are always seeking to understand both the world around us and ourselves. It's kind of a pain in the ass, really because it leads to some weird internal dialogue and story-telling on occasion. This is why meditation and mindfulness is so important. Not to achieve some woo-woo state of bliss (though good for you if you make that happen), but to pay attention to what's really going on in our own brains. What are we telling ourselves, and how is it helping or harming us?

There was an article on Forbes.com a minute ago about psychologists recommending books on mindfulness and my book *Unfuck Your Brain* was listed. While that book has done ridiculously well and seeing it recommended isn't an unusual event, having it listed as a mindfulness book was. But the psychologist who recommended it was also totally right in saying that it is essentially a book about mindfulness. Because all of therapy is at some level about mindfulness. If we aren't paying attention to what's going on in our bodies and minds we can't make the adjustments and course corrections necessary for us to heal.

So this zine is about mindfulness and meditation. You have seen the terms used interchangeably and indiscriminately, I'm sure. And while they do have overlap they are definitely not the same thing. So in this zine, I thingy-explain the differences—what a focused practice of each does for the brain, how to practice in a trauma-informed way—and *then* different types you can try to see which work best for you.

Mindfulness and Meditation

Mindfulness is the basic human ability to be aware and fully present in our own lives, to bear witness to the workings of our body and mind as well as what is going on around us. John Kabat-Zinn, likely the best known mindfulness instructor in the Western world, states that mindfulness is just *awareness.* It is the natural state of the human body, especially when we are young, but it is something we become trained out of when we developmentally get to the place where we realize we can escape our present reality and be somewhere else. In fact, researchers have found that at least half of our waking hours are spent with wandering minds.

Mindfulness does not require meditation. Mindfulness is essentially the best path we have figured out for accepting the is-ness of our lives. This isn't to say that we should take shit lying down, it's about recognizing the reality of the current moment, rather than getting so wrapped up into how we want it to be/how it should be that we get stuck. When we get stuck in how things should be we get stuck in unceasing judgement, which is not a place systemic change comes from.

Meditation, by contrast, is a formal process of focused attention and does not have to include mindfulness. Transcendental Meditation (TM) is probably the best known form of meditation that is not mindfulness-based. TM uses a monosyllabic sound as a mantra to help the mind get out of the loop of spinning thoughts (more on this in a bit). This seems like a nit-picky difference, but a mantra meditation is creating a new present moment with a specific repeated sound while mindfulness meditation is just about being in the present moment.

Mindfulness meditation is where the two meet. This is where that process of awareness is brought into the formal practice of focused attention. This doesn't mean perfect attention, but it is a process of recognizing when the mind wanders and refocusing awareness back to the present when it does, usually with some kind of anchor (the breath is the most common).

There is not a "correct" form of mindfulness, meditation, or mindfulness meditation. They all have the same goal of helping achieve a peaceful mind and manage stress, so I am including a wide variety of practices for you to experiment with.

You might have some beef with the idea of mindfulness and meditation. Which makes sense, because a lot of the breathless writing you've probably run across about it is about some kind of escape from reality into an ethereal higher consciousness. You might get the idea that you are supposed to go into meditating (or come out of it) empty-mind and completely calm. That it has to be done in a certain exact way every time, and involves some weird pretzel contortion position. And probably shaving your head and wearing saffron robes. Or whatever. And none of that is true. None of this is about changing yourself. It's the opposite: meditation and mindfulness are about meeting yourself, finding yourself, and connecting to yourself exactly as you are in the present.

Will mindfulness and/or meditation change your life? Yes. But maybe not in the ways you expect it to or hope it to. Over a decade into practice, I still don't have a calm brain. But I do have space between my brain's chatter and my reactivity. I have a different level of awareness of how I'm reacting to myself and the world. I see different choices and different paths. You may think *"that's it?"* but as a person with a loud-ass brain, I can tell you it's still life-changing.

You know why mindfulness-based therapy is so brave? Because even when we are told that we will reach down and discover our innate goodness, we are still so fearful that isn't the case. What if we are the exception? What if we are the one person too broken inside to be worthy? What if the real truth is that I am that one person who is *not* ok?

Bravery is telling that voice to fuck off. Bravery is digging deeper still, past that voice, to listen through all the chatter. And to trust that goodness is there. And you (yep, even you with your broken, hurting, scarred, and fragile insides) are still innately, beautifully, and so deeply good.

You will find that space. Keep looking.

This Is Your Brain on Mindfulness and Meditation

Mindfulness has been so well researched at this point, the research-backed benefits would be an encyclopedia in and of itself. But here are a few of the big ones.

Mindfulness has been found to:

- Positively impact overall human functioning (cognitions, emotions, physiology, and behavior)
- Improve attention and focus
- Provide greater empathy and compassion, positively impacting interpersonal behavior

- Reduce proactive interference (when old stuff we know gets in the way of new stuff we are trying to learn)
- Help manage caregiver burnout
- Help manage chronic pain (showing just as much benefit as CBT)
- Help overcome insomnia
- Help with the management of mental health issues, including depression, anxiety, and PTSD
- Increase the body's immune response

A lot of studies have been done specifically about meditation, and the results are fascinating. We have literally thousands of years of mindfulness and meditation practice documented in human history that include reported benefits of the practices. With the advent of fMRI (functional magnetic resonance imaging), we can actually *see* how mindfulness and meditation affects the functioning and even the neuroplasticity of the brain (which is the brain's ability to grow, learn, and heal damage).

When scientists look at people's brains while they meditate, they find that within a few minutes of beginning meditation, the ventromedial prefrontal cortex lights up, meaning that this part of the brain is electrically firing. This is the thinking brain, the "monkey mind," the part of the brain that tries to connect every thought to our "me-ness" and plans for the worst all the time. This is why the first few minutes of meditation feel so grunge and funky.

If you stick with it past those first uncomfortable minutes, the lateral prefrontal cortex lights up instead. This is the part of the brain that has more equilibrium. Our thoughts become less chatty and me-focused, less obsessed with potential catastrophes and more accepting of what is actually happening.

If we meditate daily (or at least really regularly) for two to three months, then our dorsomedial prefrontal cortex starts to get activated during meditation. This is the part of the brain that is related to empathy. We become more compassionate in our daily lives to ourselves and others.

Over time, meditation increases grey matter in the prefrontal cortex, which is brilliant for emotional regulation, focus, and ability to problem solve. It also thickens the hippocampus and decreases the amygdala response, which helps us stay anchored in the present (read: less likely to have our fight-flight-freeze response activated). The brains of meditators also show an increase in alpha wave activity (something people pay good money to induce with neurofeedback, hypnotherapy, and alpha stims). Meditation keeps neural connections strong and prevents atrophy. Essentially, the brain of a meditating middle-aged person is comparable to the brain of a 20 year old.

Meditation also changes the chemical structure of our body. It increases the chemicals that help us maintain calm homeostasis. GABA (gamma-aminobutyric acid), serotonin, and BDNF (brain-derived neurotrophic factor) are all chemicals that are of benefit to mood stabilization, and all are increased with meditation. Additionally, the hormones associated with stress (cortisol and adrenaline) seem to be mitigated by meditation.

This gets us back to the idea of a vagal window of tolerance. While I go into all of this in my book *Unfuck Your Body*, the shorthand version is this: the idea is for you to be thriving as much as possible, not just surviving. Our window of tolerance is our best, thinking self. It doesn't mean we don't feel some kinda way about things sometimes, but it's manageable and we are able to work with these thoughts and feelings with a measure of self-control and rationality. If we are out of that window of tolerance we are either in fight/flight mode (activated up) or freeze mode (activated down). And in either case, our bodies are engaging in survival behaviors. The only decisions we're capable of making at that point are ones that our brains perceive as helping us stay alive until the crisis is over.

More and more research is demonstrating that meditation not only helps in the moment, but helps us remain in our window of tolerance in general, not just when we are meditating, by creating positive alternations in the neural activity and connectivity of the default mode networks of the brain (the storytelling brain). This means meditation is teaching the brain to learn process-specific states of calm (all the time regulation) instead of state-specific calm (we're calm when we meditate).

If you're looking for the benefits of mindfulness and meditation, but are uncomfortable with it being tied to a particular religious or spiritual practice, you can find therapeutic programs that utilize these techniques without being tied to "something bigger." Mindfulness and meditation practices have long been used in clinical settings like therapy, and there is a huge and growing amount of research backing this up.

The two that have been around the longest and studied the most are Mindfulness-Based Stress Reduction (MBSR) which was developed by John Kabat-Zinn and his colleagues at the University of Massachusetts Medical Center and Mindfulness-Based Cognitive Therapy (MBCT), developed by Dan Siegal and his colleagues at the UCLA School of Medicine. MBSR has a more generic application and is applied to stress arising from a variety of life events including physical or mental illness. MBCT is a spin-off of MBSR, and tends to target specific conditions and vulnerabilities. It adds cognitive behavior therapy (generally considered the therapy gold standard) to MBSR in order to add focus to shifting patterns of thoughts, emotions, and behaviors that do not serve your emotional health. Other common modalities, most notably Dialectical Behavioral Therapy (DBT) and Acceptance and Commitment Therapy (ACT), are not mindfulness-based, but rely on mindfulness as a core skill.

Trauma Sensitive Practice

While mindfulness and meditation can be of huge benefit to a large number of people, it isn't magic for everyone, and may require trauma-sensitive modifications, just like any body-oriented practice. If you have a trauma history and try to sit down to meditate following any standard instructions, it's possible that it will fuck you up.

Things you may notice that are signs of dorsal and ventral vagal responses that may be associated with trauma (either fight and flight activation, or freezing up) can include:

- Prolonged, uncontrollable crying
- Shortness of breath
- Trembling
- Clenched fists
- Getting very pale or very flushed

- Excessive sweating
- Depersonalization
- Derealization
- Fear
- Panic

Having a trauma history or having a trauma response while meditating doesn't mean you can't meditate or practice mindfulness. But those of us with intense trauma histories need to have space for *choice.* This means choice to work through our trauma history in our own time and in our own way, instead of having memories flood our present moment and disrupt our lives. Traditional meditation practices encourage us to go back to the breath and to treat any triggers or activation as thinking that detracts from the present moment. Instead, a trauma-informed practice helps us lean into uncomfortable feelings without losing our zone of tolerance.

If trauma is an issue for you, here are some tips, many of them inspired by David Treleaven's book *Trauma-Sensitive Mindfulness.*

1) Recognize your internal *go* and *stop* signals (thoughts, feelings, body sensations). You don't have to sit and stew in emotional pain. Some discomfort can help us grow, but retraumatizing ourselves fixes fucking nothing. Notice what practices are helpful and which are activating. Get up and take a break when you need to, but next time stay seated just a little longer.

2) You don't have to sit in physical pain either. Take breaks when you need to or alter how you are holding

your body. Move into a more comfortable position or wiggle in place a little. While meditation (specifically mindfulness meditation) has been shown in research to be incredibly helpful to pain management, it's not supposed to be torture. Support your body in whatever ways you need to to be as comfortable as possible.

3) Meditation exercises often suggest closing your eyes. This is totally optional. If you don't feel comfortable with your eyes closed in the environment you're in, leave them open. Or start with a soft gaze as a step towards closing your eyes.

4) If your practice involves attending a class, talk to the teacher. If there is any hands-on component (like if your practice involves yoga or tai chi), you can tell them not to provide physical adjustments (meaning, not to touch you).

Just like with everything else regarding *your* mental and physical health, listen to your body more than you listen to me. Don't do things that are awful and upsetting for you. Meditation is a chance to work through crap without being overactivated. So if you are overactivated by something, it may not be for you, at least not right now.

How to do Mindfulness and Meditation

The rest of this zine is devoted to giving you a taste of some of the variety of practices to see which resonate best with you. There is meditation without mindfulness, mindfulness without meditation, and practices that incorporate both.

The fact that there are such a wide variety of practices out there that have demonstrated effectiveness is really good news. If you have had bad experience with any practice in the past, it means there are a variety of other methods you can experiment with.

Let's try some new stuff, yeah?

Basic Mindfulness Meditation Instructions

This is the classic, go-to mindfulness based meditation that uses breath as the anchor to the present moment.

- Settle in a comfortable position. Sitting with an aligned back is the classic method (either on a cushion or in a straight backed chair) but if that isn't a position you can get into or maintain, no worries—settle your body to be as presence-focused as possible.

- Bring your awareness to the physical sensations of your body. Where do you feel the pressure of your body making contact with your chair, bed, or floor? What other sensations (like air, temperature, texture) do you notice? Spend a minute or two noticing those sensations.

- Now bring your awareness to your lower abdomen, recognizing the sensations of your breath moving in and out of your body. You can place a hand on your abdomen to help you feel the sensation if you are struggling to make that connection if that's helpful. Notice your abdominal wall stretching and inflating with each in-breath and gently deflating with each out breath.

- Continue to follow the breath in and out, giving yourself permission to just be in the experience of your breath.

- Eventually (probably sooner rather than later) you will notice that your mind is wandering. You start daydreaming, planning, getting consumed with other thoughts. My brain likes to sing songs and make shopping lists, personally. This is what brains do. It doesn't make you a mindful meditation failure. Just when you notice that you're doing it, label it "thinking" and focus back on the breath.

- Bring curiosity and patience to your wanderings, rather than frustration. Notice what was going on and return to the breath.

Most research demonstrates that 15 minutes of practice is the amount of time it takes to gain the benefits of mindfulness meditation. If you can't tolerate it for that long, that's also okay. Practice working up to it. If you find that it's helpful and want to extend time out further that's also great, but not required.

Mindfully Eating a Raisin

This mindful eating practice is a classic MBSR (mindfulness-based stress reduction) technique. It gives you a different element to focus on, other than your breath.

- Place a few raisins in your hand. And no you don't have to use raisins, any food will do. I've found that even people who don't like raisins are not bothered by them in this exercise. But if they really gross you out, grab something else.

- Pretend this is your first day on the planet. This is a new food that you have never seen before, and you are an alien explorer that is going to make scientific study of raisins and raisin-ness. Use all five of your senses to explore it. Turn it around with your fingers, notice the color, the tactical sensations. How does it fold or reflect light? What does it smell like when you hold it up to your nose? Does it make any sound if you apply pressure?

- You will start having thoughts of the "Why am I doing this? This is fucking weird" variety. Totally normal. Just recognize them as a thought you are having and bring yourself back to the activity.

- Bring the object slowly to your mouth. Notice how automatic it is for your hand to bring nourishment up to your mouth. Notice whatever anticipation you are experiencing. Is your mouth watering? Gently place the raisin on your tongue without biting down. Explore the sensation of the raisin in your mouth.

- When you are ready, bite down. Notice the taste that is released when doing so. Notice how you habitually move it to one side of your mouth over another. Slowly chew the raisin. Notice how it changes in texture and flavor as you chew. When you feel ready to swallow, notice your conscious intention to do so. Pay attention to the sensation of it moving down your throat to your esophagus.

How did the experience of eating differ when you did so mindfully? What did you notice? What did you enjoy? What was uncomfortable?

Metta Meditation

Metta loosely translates as *loving-kindness.* In essence, it's a focus of general goodwill, friendliness, and open-heartedness. It's a way of engaging in the world without all shields up, feeling defensive and ill at ease.

A metta meditation involves focusing not just on the breath, but on a series of healing statements about yourself, another person or group of people, or the world.

The original texts from the Buddha on metta (as translated from *The Discourse on Loving-Kindness)* is:

> *Wishing: In gladness and in safety, may all beings be at ease.*
>
> *Whatever living beings there may be, omitting none*
>
> *Let none deceive another, or despise any being in any state*
>
> *Let none through anger or ill will wish harm upon another.*

These statements have an archaic language (don't worry, we're gonna use a more modern format), but speak to universal human struggles across time. Specifically, the harm we experience just by being a human living in an imperfect world, and the continued harm (suffering) that we impose on ourselves in the process. Metta meditation allows us to work with the feelings we avoid the most, like aversion and despair. The Buddha stated that by working with uncomfortable emotions, we can transform them into something that serves us better.

When we don't like someone, doing a metta meditation on their behalf feels gross. My meditation instructor encourages focusing on the easiest people first, the people or living things we love and adore (yes, it can absolutely be your pup or your favorite tree in the park if you aren't feeling particularly people-y). After that, we can move to the people who are a little more sketch, and finally to the people we consider the most difficult as we build tools to release what about them creates toxic emotions within us.

Also, we should offer metta to ourselves. Self-hatred is far more common than hatred of others. Buddhist meditation instructor Sharon Salzberg discusses how this is a super common in Western culture as an offset of systemic oppression (defined by bell hooks as "imperialist white supremacist capitalist patriarchy"). Because no matter what set of circumstances or privileges we have accessed, no one measures up to these standards. We all struggle with not-enoughness and feel a continuous need to earn our space in the world, rather than recognizing that we deserve by the sheer fact that we are human.

Here are some more modernized metta meditation statements that you can use in your own practice, that are used more often now than the Buddha's originals. You can say these out loud or think them in your head, timed with your breath. Where there is a blank you insert "I" or "my" for doing metta for yourself, "you" or the name of the person you are focusing on, or "all" meaning the entirety of sentient beings.

- May _____ be protected and safe from harm from others
- May______be protected and safe from self-inflicted harm
- May _____ be happy
- May _____ body support the practice of loving awareness
- May _____ be free from anxiety
- May _____ be free from anger
- May______be free from fear
- May______love themself/themselves exactly as they are
- May _____ be free from suffering
- May _____ find peace in the world
- May _____ find balance between attachment and apathy

Mantra Meditation

Using a mantra to meditate is the best known form of meditation that isn't mindfulness based. In Sanskrit, *man* translates to "mind," and *tra* means "to free from." Mantras are used as a tool to free the mind (or to be freed from the mind). They help break the cycle of spinning thoughts that lead to anxiety, self-doubt and the like. Transcendental Meditation, which relies on mantras, got really big when Maharishi Mahesh Yogi brought the ancient technique to the US.

As with other practices that have spiritual roots, researchers in the US were interested in how the techniques themselves, outside a cultural context, can alter physical and mentals states. Since the 1970s, Herbert Benson, professor of medicine at Harvard Medical School and founder of the Benson-Henry Institute for Mind Body Medicine at Massachusetts General Hospital, has studied what creates that meditative state, which he termed "the relaxation response" (with a bestselling book by the same name).

Benson has experimented with subjects repeating Sanskrit mantras as well as nonreligious words, such as "one." He's found that regardless of what the practitioner repeats, the word or phrase has nearly the same effects: relaxation and the ability to better cope with life's unexpected stressors. Mantras actually soothe the default mode of the brain, keeping it from going into storytelling mode and creating anxious thoughts.

Sanskrit chanting is often part of many practices, including different branches of yoga. The sanskrit often has complex meanings beyond the literal translations. I've found that learning the relevance and meaning behind mantras like *om mani padme hum* lends depth to my practice. But, mantras in any language have the same effect. You can chant any contemplative expression from your faith system (like "Hail Mary, full of grace") or something more generally spiritual (like "I am Divine Love"), or any secular humanist phrase, and gain the same default mode benefit. Or maybe there is a certain mantra about your path of healing that you want to use.

Once you've decided on a mantra, find your comfy place and set a timer for yourself. Start with a few deep breaths and then start chanting your mantra (in your head is fine, outloud voice is also fine). If you catch your thoughts wandering, bring them back to the mantra.

Meditation in Motion

What we often refer to as "walking meditation" is really just "meditation in motion." Whatever device you may use for mobility will become part of the process.

- Find an unobstructed space in which you can move back and forth in a reasonably straight line for about ten feet (yes, you can also do a greater distance). If you are walking and are able to do so barefoot (and it's an area that is safe for you to be barefoot), you may find it helpful to gain more awareness of how your body creates balance for movement.

- If you are walking, bring your attention to your feet, shifting your weight from side to side and front to back, as far as you are comfortably able to do so. Lift your head and chest so you are facing forward, let your shoulders drop away from your ears. You can clasp your hands behind your back, hold them in front of you, or let them hang loosely at your side.

- Lift up one of your legs. It doesn't matter which, but take notice. Pay attention to how your weight shifts in your body when you do so. What does the other side of your body need to do to hold your full weight? Move your lifted foot forward, then place your heel on the ground and roll the rest of your foot down, ending with your toes. Pay attention to how your other foot begins to lift and move forward as well. Bring that foot forward and repeat.

- If you use a device for mobility, focus your attention on the sensations of movement. Connect the sensation of using your hands to connect to the mobility support and guide you forward. Feel the sensation of moving forward and your connection of being embodied and supported in that experience. If you are using a chair that relies on voice, facial expression identification, or the like, focus on how you engage your body and connect to the chair to create movement. What shifts do you feel physically and energetically?

- No matter how you create movement, your mind will wander as minds like to do. As your attention wanders off, you can bring yourself back to present practice with the thought of "attention engagement forward" or an anchoring reminder of your choice.

- When you come to the end of your path (unless it was a circle to begin with), turn fully around, face the direction from which you came, and start over. If you are moving in a circular shape, simply notice that you have completed one full round.

Meditation on the Soles of the Feet

This particular practice has been shown to be really beneficial for the management of aggression and anger.

- If you are standing, stand in whatever relaxed posture is most natural for you.
- If you are sitting, sit comfortably with the soles of your feet flat on the floor or another surface.
- Breathe normally. You don't have to do deep belly breaths or anything outside of how you regularly breathe.
- Now, think back on an incident that made you very angry. Stay with that anger. Let the angry thoughts flow through your mind without trying to stop them. You may notice your heart rate or breathing go up as you remember that anger.
- Now, shift all your attention to the soles of your feet.
- Slowly, move your toes, feel your shoes covering your feet, feel the texture of your socks or hose, the curve of your arch, and the heels of your feet against the back of your shoes. If you do not have shoes on, feel the floor or carpet with the soles of your feet.
- Keep breathing naturally and focus on the soles of your feet until you feel calm and the physical signs of anger dissipate, this will take probably 10 to 15 minutes.
- Slowly come out of your meditation, sit quietly for a few moments, and then resume your daily activities.

Cognitive Defusion

Remember earlier when I talked about how we can practice mindfulness without doing so in the form of meditation? And how some forms of therapy aren't mindfulness-based but still center mindfulness as a core skill? Cognitive defusion is a technique from Acceptance and Commitment Therapy (ACT) that focuses on mindfulness in managing being overwhelmed, without having to sit on a cushion with it. As with the other practices listed here, this is one I use with clients regularly.

This skill is designed to help manage thoughts that are painful, overwhelming, unkind, or unhelpful. We tend to over identify (fuse) with our thoughts, so thinking something like "I'm terrible" or "I don't deserve love" can become the truths we operate within unless we approach them with mindfulness.

- Start by identifying a hurtful self-criticism that you want to work with. If you can shorten it into a phrase or single sentence, it's easier to work with than a rambling paragraph of self-recrimination (which is my personal speciality).
- Let yourself engage with the thought rather than try to push it away. You can repeat it to yourself mentally, or verbalize it out loud.
- Now add this modifier in front of it: "I'm having the thought that..." so "I don't deserve love" becomes "I'm having the thought that I don't deserve love."

- Now take another step away from it by adding "I notice…" so we are now at "I notice I'm having the thought that I don't deserve love."
- It may be wordy and complex at first, but with some practice you may be able to shorten it into a sentence that really gets at the heart of the issue.
- Now reflect on whatever mental shifts you noticed as you defused the thought by recognizing it as an experience your brain was having instead of as your life operating instructions. What did you notice?

Mindfulness and Pain Management

Mindfulness for pain, whether acute or chronic, doesn't mean learning to ignore the pain so we can go about our day (let's be real, we are already way too good at that). Trying to escape pain just gets us more ensnared in the long run. When we feel what's real in the present rather than trying to hide from it, we are more awake and alive to reality. It's how we bear witness to reality, to be curious and compassionate rather than shaming and blaming or prickly and protective.

You can use mindfulness to specifically train your brain to cope with pain by recognizing its existence rather than trying to avoid it completely or getting swallowed whole by it.

When we hurt, our breathing tends to get shallow, in an attempt to avoid the pain. We can breathe into and through the pain as a form of mindful recognition, allowing the pain to speak to us and pass through.

Mindfulness can also include "conscious distraction" which seems like a contradictory statement, but if we start with attention, we can then make a decision to feel into our pain or to let ourselves carve out a break from it which is far different from "ignore ignore ignore."

We can also breathe into the places that are not in pain, focusing on whatever areas of our body are not experiencing pain at this moment, even if it's just the middle toe of your left foot.

If the pain is wildfire, you can even choose a focal point outside the body and declare it your "no-pain zone" to focus on while breathing deeply. This gives the nervous system some relief from its constant messaging. I had a college professor that started each class with a candle and a vase of flowers as our focal point in the middle of the room. Nowadays, I have a tattoo on my right wrist that serves as my focal point / anchor / reminder to be present.

Humming for Migraines

Tony Bateson, a chronic migraine sufferer, recognized that his migraines dissipated when he ranted and raved out loud. So he started studying, first of all, how that could possibly be, and second of all, if he could gain the same effect without the yelly part. He found a good deal of literature on sound healing and came up with the hypothesis that humming at a particular frequency was the part that disrupted the headaches. He began to play with the technique, particularly with mantra meditation, and came up with something that has helped others.

Others have since studied what he came up with and stated that it makes sense. Pain takes control of our brain oscillations (brain waves) and if we use an acoustic that creates an oscillation of the opposite frequencing as the pain oscillation, it would neutralize. Acoustic frequencies, like mantras, have been shown to change the brain. So electrophysiologists think it may help with other pain as well.

The frequency Bateson found most effective to hum is 140 hz, which is essentially a low C sharp. My Buddhist-y and yoga-y readers will recognize this as the same tone as the chanted OM (which is also known as the sound of creation). If you are trying to find that frequency, look for a YouTube video so you don't have to invest in a pitch pipe to get it right. You are going to hum with your upper and lower jaw held together, teeth touching, but not a clenched jaw. Try to keep the hum as regular a rhythm as possible.

- Hum for 10 seconds
- Take a deep breath in through the nose
- On the exhale, hum again for 10 seconds
- Repeat for 9 more cycles (ten cycles total of hums)
- Rest for two minutes
- Repeat the sequence (ten cycles and two minutes of rest)
- Then rest for 10 minutes before going about your day